INSIDE THE HEAD OF AN ASPERGER

René Maurice Dereumaux

INSIDE THE HEAD OF AN ASPERGER

Max Milo
TÉMOIGNAGES

www.maxmilo.com
ISBN: 978-2-31501-415-6

Inside the head of an Asperger

For as long as I can remember, I've had the impression of living differently from others. Of the image of being different that they reflect back to me. That I feel by force… By force…

I imagine this other person living in a kind of dream, evolving in a language that's foreign to me. As if he lives in a *dream*. And I, disturbed, am inhabited by a drama. The same letters, slightly altered, and because of this anagram, you're thrown into a totally different environment. Incomprehensible, nightmarish… There's no translation, no reading grid, because no one is likely to know both languages…

Even if the challenge of getting you into the head of an Asperger's-type autistic person is a gamble, not to try would have been heartbreaking…

"Curious" is a term I've often been called.

I found it flattering, and for someone considered to be egocentric, I confess I readily accepted it, acknowledging that I frequently found myself in a state of persistent questioning. Except that, being unable to detect a certain form of irony, or even mockery in the tone used by the person evaluating me, I naively contented myself with the original meaning of the word… It was only when I was older that I discovered that "curious" was polysemous… If in the active sense "curious" means to feel interest in something, in the passive sense it expresses someone who arouses strangeness, weirdness!

I can assure you that it's not always pleasant to be looked at as a curious beast! By people close to you, as well as those further away! This painful experience has prompted me to be much more vigilant about the meaning of words and expressions I hear and use, and to take an interest in semasiology in particular.

Their eyes don't seem so dark to me, and even if they don't generally throw aggression at me, I don't always manage to hold their gaze... I run away from them.

Mostly from myself...

At times, without any rational necessity, my upper eyelids are lowered as if each of their respective eyelashes were wrapped around a dumbbell! Is this a necessary discomfort to remind me of my otherness?

But fortunately for the other person, my Asperger's Autism Spectrum Disorder (ASD) is not contagious! Fear not!

In a society where marketing is king, everyone tries to convey the most positive image of themselves possible… My coach is full of dents… Me, who is exclusively focused on a single interest: cars. Not when it comes to buying a car—the act of buying a car seems pointless to me—but when it comes to reading magazines and specialized websites, and observing the cars on the street in detail… I have to admit that I'm constantly making connections with this obsession, even if it means annoying those around me… And while I admit that I don't get tired of endlessly repeating the same words on the same subject, this isn't always the case for those who are subjected to my phrases!

Roya Valley, summer 2017, discovering the world of the wolf, whose life fascinates me in certain ways: mysterious eyes, profound solitude, an animal that is worried, hunted and chased. The guide talks in detail about the Alpha couple who dominate those who live in a pack. I cut him off to point out that the male is the Alpha Romeo and the female the Alpha Juliet...

Feeling bad about myself. Would changing it be enough to change me?

This skin that's not tight enough, that hurts if you squeeze it just a little too hard, even with kindness. A skin that refuses to be naked under the sun, in seawater, under the comforter… That avoids all contact, especially conventional handshakes…

For whom the slightest label on an item of clothing causes discomfort that can become obsessive. A skin of sorrow!

If it's sometimes appropriate for me to have a sensitivity on the surface of my skin, I understand it in the Baudelairian approach of those that hurt, as in the last three lines of *Remords posthumes*:

> *[Le tombeau] Te dira: "Que vous sert, courtisane imparfaite,*
> *Not to have known what the dead mourn?"*
> *—And the worm will gnaw at your skin like remorse.*

Paradoxically, physical contact with an animal—cat, dog, horse or even the bark of a tree—calms me down, as if the bad tensions inside me were suddenly and wonderfully absorbed, as if neutralized.

And how are we to understand the expression "to have someone in your skin" when we feel so badly in our own?

Because long before this stage, you have to be seductive, and so impose on yourself a reduction of who you really are... Then you have to dress up in a literal as well as figurative definition, polishing yourself up like a dandy, me being a kind of Handicapped person... Before you have to undress, and find yourself skin against skin...

Not easy!

Can we go straight to the post-liminaries?

Jean-Jacques Rousseau puts forward a powerful idea in his *Discourse on Sciences and Arts*, which raises one of the central themes of his philosophy: "Man is born naturally good and happy; it is society that corrupts him and makes him unhappy." Beyond the idea of refuting the notion of original sin, what appeals to me about Rousseau is the danger that society represents for the individual, contact with others. When the skin can't play its role as a bulwark, from the outside in, the energy deployed is unrestrained. Probably magnificent in a positive approach, certainly devastating in the opposite case. A skin so thin that the other can easily penetrate the depths of your being. Hence, more or less unconsciously, the need to withdraw in order to protect yourself. An Asperger-type autistic person is less prepared, less protected, ar mé in the face of others, in the face of potential aggression. And even if the aggressiveness felt is perhaps not always intentional, or even real, the tension is nevertheless very high. So avoiding meetings, parties, clubs and associations can be a kind of salutary protection. One only has to be familiar with Stockholm syndrome, and measure the naivety and speed with which solid neurotypicals can transform themselves, to wonder?

After Jean-Pierre Claris de Florian's cricket realizes that children are cruelly tearing apart the butterfly whose freedom and beauty he had just envied, he finally understands that "To live happily, let's live hidden". This is why the environment seems to me to be a determining factor. Undermining. And if I also like Tolstoy's phrase: "As long as there are slaughte-rhouses, there will be battlefields", it's because it evokes the great danger of an Asperger's type autistic *person's peaurosity...*

Anger is an integral part of my character, my characteristics...

Often unexpected by those around me and by myself. Almost always unjustified after the fact. At the moment of its expression, it's unlikely to cease to exist... I'm totally inhabited by it. In crescendo, D, E, F, G, A, B...

It's the damage her verbal outrages cause to those who suffer them that makes me aware of her absurdity. Of my own... The explanation put forward by psychiatrists is that Asperger's sufferers don't know empathy, so I wouldn't be at all aware of the pain I might cause the other person through my hurtful words...

"What an excuse!" I've been cheekily told!

Flat excuses aren't enough, and neither are *anfractuous* ones, so from now on I try with great difficulty to avoid the traps set for me by this formidable enemy, by being almost constantly vigilant in the areas she appreciates: the delicate temperature of dishes, a ridiculous delay on the part of the other person, a phrase felt to be hurtful because it's often misunderstood, a light experienced as too bright, a smell considered too strong, a noise judged too violent…

In fact, it can be found anywhere! Anything can suddenly become a pretext for a *casus belli*! And that's the tragedy, because so many good times have been stupidly ruined! Irreversibly…

How can I understand that all too often sounds come to me with the same intensity, in such a way that I can't select them, prioritize them, causing a total cacophony that prevents me from sorting things out and therefore deciding when I can intervene or keep quiet?... Knowing that when I speak, apart from on the subject of cars, I'm very frequently reproached for expressing what I think, for using a tone of voice remptoire, even *sarcaustic*!... And what can I say about this stupidity of putting inordinate pressure on those around me to be not on time, but on the minute! For a reserved table in a restaurant, and thus spoil a lovely family moment!... Or that spotlight that lights up my face and that I receive like a permanent flash! Why doesn't anyone smell the chlorine that disturbs me to the point of obsession?

Because I'm probably different, and I feel a great violence in what neurotypicals seem to accept so easily...

If, *in hindsight*, I can intellectually understand that it's not the noise that bothers me, but rather the idea that I have of it, in the moment I'm as if invaded by it, without any hindsight. Like Nietzsche's cow, which, living in the immediacy of the grass, cannot be aware of its opacity, I stupidly experience this noise... this smell... this light...

Or how to feed my turpitudes...

Boredom has been my faithful companion for a long time. The possessive is not excessive! For the Greeks, there are several characteristics of time: Chronos, the classic, mechanical one, that of the watch. Kairos, more subtle, with different thicknesses and durations. It's non-linear. Then there's Aîon, cyclical time. However, it wasn't until 1905 that Einstein, in his theory of special relativity, scientifically shattered the idea that time is a universal constant...

Boredom exists when you become aware that time is not passing. When you're stuck in an interminable wait that never seems to end. In a kind of old-fashioned Kairos with a broken elastic band! A singular atemporality that couldn't care less about social time values.

Some people dread the finitude of life, but perhaps they've never known boredom?

The heaviness of time that seems to stand still, that gives me the unpleasant feeling of going round in circles, of treading water. Imprisoned. Imprisoned. I was already very bored at the local school. At family gatherings *too*. After the baccalaureate, I preferred to stop time wasting away. Which was losing me…

As I embarked on my so-called active life, I soon found the man for whom I had been an unwilling sidekick. It was only at the dawn of my forties, overcome by a feeling of weariness in my job for which the shareholders were nonetheless satisfied, and also because my son was enjoying his studies and made me want to, that I decided to take up studies myself. In the space of five years, I entered HEC for an Executive MBA, defended a thesis in management and passed a master's degree in diplomacy...

No glory! Just more boredom, which at least had the virtue of locking me in on myself, and thus preventing anyone from discovering a certain kind of naivety, unthinkable in this type of environment, which is all too often heavily elitist.

I haven't formed any relationships in all these years! I've also published three books.

Nevertheless, I decided to continue along the path of *Long Life Learning*.

For another five years, I took psychoanalysis courses, combined with clinical and then didactic analysis.

During the last year, in 2015, still inhabited by a deep sense of boredom, at a conference my attention was drawn to a subject dealing with Autistic Spectrum Disorder, more specifically of the Asperger's type.

Mention was made of the impossibility of making friends, selective mutism, inability to empathize, lack of eye contact with others, being active but odd, lack of leisure activities, the practice of tailor-made daily routines, literal interpretations, an excellent ability to recognize shapes, poor motor skills!!!!

How could this speaker know me so well? To express, to detail what I had never before dared reveal except to myself!

For more than a year, I kept on:

—Interviews: clinical interviews with psychiatrists from the CRA (Centre Ressources Autistes) to gather clinical information on the three areas making up the symptoms of the autistic triad:

—Disorders of reciprocal social interaction.

—Verbal and non-verbal communication disorders.

—Restricted interests and repetitive behaviors.

—To answer questionnaires and carry out examinations:

AQ: Autistic Quotient.

EQ: Empathy Quotient.

SQ-R: Revised Methodic Quotient.

—To be filmed at length with my consent.

—To undergo tests and trials, including the ADOS: a tiring test specific to autism.

My wife was seen twice at the CRA by the same highly professional doctors as myself, for a clinical interview and to answer precise questions. She will be affected! An environment of autistic children, precise questions both about our daily lives and our relationships, a confrontation with a difficult reality…

The result will fall in 2016 in the form of an eleven-page report:

"The questionnaires, the ADOS and the clinical presentation are concordant and allow us to make a diagnosis of Autistic Spectrum Disorder (ASD according to the DSM-V), of the Asperger Syndrome type"…

The DSM stands for *Diagnostic and Statistical Manual of Mental Disorder*, and is the international reference work published by the APA, the American Psychiatric

Association, which describes and classifies mental disorders. The latest publication, the fifth, dates from 2013.

I had to wait fifty-seven *horrible years* to finally be recognized in my singularity as an Asperger's sufferer, albeit with a giftedness that was confirmed at the same time.

As announced by the psychiatrist in charge of my case: this assessment is an explanation, not an excuse... Knowing that the CRA told me that, as an adult, I would not be offered any support, any follow-up, any help! Because, apart from diagnosis, the center exists exclusively for children and teenagers...

After filling out a complete file with the invaluable help of the CRA, the Maison départementale des personnes handicapées issued me with an RQTH (Recognition as a

Disabled Worker) some eight months later! Confusing terminology! Disconcerting... While specifying my freedom to inform my employer or not!... Exclusive disjunction but, for it to be expressed, an employer would still have to be interested in this type of atypical profile with the private "A" for NeuroAtypical. Abnormal.

Strangely enough, as someone who's a bit weird, I experienced these moments of discovery of my syndrome as no nuyeux! Exhilarating even!

Confucian saying: "You have two lives, and the second begins when you realize you only have one! Let me rectify that for myself: "You have two lives, and the second begins when you realize you have Asperger's autism."

Annus mirabilis?

Certain letters and numbers are of particular interest to me.

Let's take the "i", it seems to me like a haloed stem, a pretty flower... I enjoy using it on purpose or looking for it in a conversation in which I may or may not be taking part... When you hear invincibility or invisibility, what a pleasure! Indivisibility, the must-have! A real bouquet that the speaker offers you with all the more generosity because he's not aware of it... Sometimes certain "ï"s have a double head, they're bizarre, as if they were suffering from ambiguity, paranoia! Or sometimes they don a hat, respecting an Elder, a Master! As for the English, they have a very precise approach to the spirit of this letter, choosing it as their "I" who dares to cry out his torment!

I'm wary of the letter that precedes it in the arbitrary classification of the alphabet.

A letter that's pronounced like a barbaric weapon, that's sometimes sucked in and doesn't inspire me too much. It *hombres* the letters that follow it: homme, honneur, histoire... or hides them: haïr, harceler, hitler, horion, hié rarchie... it eclipses the horizon, and worse, it corresponds to a fearsomely devastating bomb... As a coffee substitute, I appreciate chicory... From the South!

Coupled with the charmingly curved third letter of the alphabet, the resulting digram allows the "h" of the human word to nestle in, to forget itself, as when we find ourselves during such warm moments in the close company of someone we cherish...

Endowed with an extravagant richness, the "x" appeals to me greatly... In upper case it corresponds exclusively to the number 10, in lower case it symbolizes the mathematical unknown whose solution we must discover among billions of digits! Some women give birth under it... A multitude of legal proceedings have been opened against him! It also signifies a crossover, as in a chiasmus or a cross. Thanks to it, figures and numbers multiply, ad infinitum. Il était une fois, deux fois, trois fois... For a karyotype, it's the symbol of the female sex, part of whose population is sacrificed to satisfy the frustrations of millions of horny people who consult sites dedicated to her, representing a multi-billion euro industry... It's quite fanciful and is pronounced differently depending on the word: For example, "tax", "sixth", "sixty"... In some words, it is used in the singular, as if to show us the need to be plural, so that both the signi fiant and the signified can be expressed, as in jealous, venomous or bellicose. Ticklish, amorous too...

Still, the world would be a much nicer place if everyone felt fully eureu, without andicap...

The letter "l" interests me when it splits, because with just one letter "l" I feel like I'm going round in circles, whereas with two "l"s I can *take off* like a butterfly, a bee, a swallow... And what about the dragonfly! Delicious illusions promising a plural, and therefore immortal, existence...

The letter "z" is probably the one for which I have the most sympathy. It corresponds to my hero Zorro! When I see a "z" in a word, I always see it as the signature of my favorite character! Especially when it corresponds to a number! What a magnificent alliance: zero, eleven, twelve, thirteen… Two "z "s in the same word being top: pizza, jazz, puzzle, grizzly, even zizanie… I've seen the Spanish fox dozens of times in the seventy-eight twenty-five-minute episodes plus the four fifty-minute episodes, first in black and white then colorized. I still watch them very frequently.

The letter "o" is very interesting, even surprising, because it also responds to the number 0, a pretty circle that can be written freely with a letter or a number! When a being is congratulated with *Good Job*, *Good Man*, *Good Girl*, *Good Dog*… I translate it into *Boons*, and paradoxically, the more zeros you find in *Boons*, the more the being progresses! A kind of Booster… Cool!

The number 3 delights me especially when thought of in the English language, a liberating number… I love to trinitize my wife, our son and me by secretly repeating the same thoughts 3 times, or the same words 3 times, or the same gestures 3 times…

The 8 enchants me! What a joy to be able to trace an 8 on paper, sand, snow. In space! Whether it's vertical or horizontal, Bernouilli's lemniscate symbolizing infinity expresses itself admirably, since even by drawing it, we understand that we can cover this infinity infinitely… In cosmology, there is spatial infinity and temporal infinity. As for spatial infinity, although astrophysics has very powerful mathematical and technical resources at its disposal, it nevertheless comes up against metaphysics which, in its etymological approach, marks our anthropic limits… So beyond our difficult physical realities as poor humans, how can we not imagine the existence of a secret passage to reach the

8th heaven, already thanks to the drawing of a perfect 8...

The 9 is also astonishing, three times more liberating than the 3! In Voltaire's language, it gives the other numbers an old-fashioned look, and is the last single-digit rampart in the decimal system. It also corresponds to the *ninth* month of gestation for humans... Can an Asperger's-type autistic person be someone who counts? Someone you can count on?

Observing letters and numbers is a special way for me to seek out a stimulus, often a detail, that will capture my attention and occupy my mind. To take my mind off things, even for a moment... Are you going off in all directions?

Take a "z" and place it in the center. On each side you place an "o", an "i", an "a", an "r" and then, after paradoxically separating a short copulative conjunction expressing a link, you obtain the word "artiozoan" which qualifies and designates any animal whose characteristic is bilateral symmetry like that of vertebrates, allowing movement in a single direction…

Even as a child, these gymnastics kept my mind busy. They reassured me a little… Even today…

These exercises, which consume an enormous amount of energy and are sometimes even exhausting, are a kind of cuddly toy, a virtual transitional object that I create for myself between a distant and aggressive outside world and a very personal inside world… A fact that may shed some light on how and why we can be sometimes creative: as we have a naively childish way of looking at the outside world, and we absolutely must hide this particular disposition to avoid the inevitable mockery and ridicule, all the more hurtful as they are often incomprehensible, so we invent another universe for ourselves. A universe so different from that of Neurotypicals that we have to hide it deep down inside! Even if it's full of numbers and letters, it's ours. That's why we don't want to get out!

In fact, this universe is us. And at this point, we can't get out...

Although it seems to be agreed that I was verbally and intellectually precocious, in everyday life I proved to be the opposite of Neurotypiques: I couldn't tie my shoes or dress myself properly. I was catastrophically clumsy in all my movements, whether I was pouring milk into a bowl, putting jam on a slice of bread, or putting the dishes away...

Even today... Acting as if...

En compagnie de l'autre is not the right expression for me, not with the other, but rather in the presence of the other, whom I need not to understand, but to observe and try to copy. Not to make my characteristics disappear, which is impossible, but to hope to reduce their visibility.

Knowing that imitating the other is limited by a lack of authenticity, which only reinforces an already naturally present awkwardness... So I might as well not see it!

The other sometimes plays the same game. He's discovered a quirk about me and, under the guise of education, prefers to ignore it. Ignore me. Non-Asperger autistic people don't have to worry about this too much, as they're quickly classified by the Neurotypicals. For them, the situation is much clearer. On this subject, isn't it shocking to compare autistic and Asperger-type autistic people by integrating a scale that would qualify one as high-level?

And the other?

Shamefully ridiculous...

Of course, it may seem important to list and segment.

But also to name. Correctly. Which means being correct with the person being named...

Under the same heading of autism, you'll find people affected by this disease at its most cruel, with intellectual deficiencies in over 40% of cases!

But how can you lump people together under the same umbrella term:

—with an IQ below 70, with others who combine Asperger's and giftedness, and whose IQ peaks at over 130!...

—whose life expectancy is reduced by seventeen years, whereas that of Aspergers is the national average!

How can this be?

Shakira's video clip is on TV. In French, it should be called "Chatte qui sourit"...

In ancient Rome, *otium* was a term used to describe the free time that people could devote to their hobbies, while *negotium* corresponded to the constraints associated with more material obligations... Seneca, a Stoic, attributed many virtues to *otium* in the sense that it favored their development.

Just as in the word weather you find summer, it's amusing to note that in the word *negotium* we find *otium*, as if it too represented hope for the remaining time-spaces. A kind of optimum.

What appeals to me about *otium* is its correspondence with a contemplative approach, a kind of spectacle of life. The mind wanders, without opium... Spectator. Not *a spectator*! Nor *Spectracteur*! Still less *Spectradetractor...*

Phew! The gong that saves me from my trivialities...

Let's go back to the *hypernegotiumized* neurotypicals and punctually leave behind this bovarysm and its characteristic frustration of someone who naively thinks he can fulfill himself, or even blossom, in a universe he has solitarily built for himself...

To feel liberated! If only for a moment!

Please, please, please...

Not knowing which personal pronoun is singular or plural...

Routine reassures me. It's my hiding place. Whether it manifests itself in my words, my gestures or my schedule, it's always welcome. It reassures me. Getting up, eating, going to bed, always at the same time, in the same place…

Without it, I feel at a loss, lost, and a horrible anxiety takes possession of me, an intense tension whenever I find myself confronted with a situation contrary to my habits, which can be described as cognitive dissonance, and which can sometimes lead to unfounded anger for the other person, or more often to withdrawal: fists clenched, jaw clenched, eyes seemingly terribly dark… I loathe change, especially last-minute, unforeseen change!

I have to admit that my life has been built on habits, rituals and length:

—I've been married for over thirty-four years to a devoted wife who, according to psychiatrists, has skilfully adapted to who I am, accommodating me by setting up a subtle *modus vivendi* that protects me, protects us. She's very attentive and manages the entire domestic life of our household: meals, shopping, maintenance, bank accounts, contracts, choice of clothes…, which reduces the tensions I might con arise if I had to face such a constraint;

—I worked for the same employer for over twenty-four years before he thanked me in the sense that he terminated my services, but not in the sense that some of those close to me feel that he could have expressed a little gratitude to me;

—I run a lot, more than two thousand kilometers a year with the same brand of shoes for more than twenty years;

—I read for over six hours every day, mainly essays and articles on philosophy, religion, history and politics. Through these readings, I also try to understand how neurotypicals can think;

—I devour everything to do with cars;

—In a family restaurant that my wife and I enjoy, the waiter always assigns us the same table. As soon as we arrive, he brings me the tomato juice as an aperitif, followed by the starter, main course and dessert, which have been the same for me for over twenty years…

A lover of *neologisms*, I consider this life to be appalling, if only because I'm not really independent in my daily life: when choosing clothes, when preparing a meal, when making purchases… I've never once gone into a store to make a purchase for myself. Not even a treat … I see two main reasons for this:

—The pleasure principle is a distant notion as far as I'm concerned, different from that expressed by Neurotypicals, who get excited about a new smartphone, an outing with friends, a TV series. I prefer solitude and tranquillity, which at least have the merit of not adding stress to already heavy stress…

—Choice implies deprivation, and it's painful for me to have to choose, because I keep coming back to the choice or non-choice, and this for hours, days… The benefit of choice cannot compensate for the conflict linked to abandoning the non-choice! Refusing to choose is a form of resistance to change, and allows me to avoid the anguish that systematically follows.

But God is also confronted with choice, because he has to choose among all that is allowed to him. So for him too, not everything is always possible. The difference is that if he's not Asperger's, he assumes his non-choice. But if God is Asperger's, then he can't choose and prefers to leave the dilemma to humans…

What were the circumstances that enabled or favored this condition?

There must have been a contest! With some very worthy candidates. Each wanting to shine, to be on the podium. Whatever it takes! Cost me…

A premature birth. By forceps… Fate had to be forced, or how to make a mockery of something you can't do *much* about!

Hans Asperger and Lorna Wing, who don't live in my village. Civil servant teachers, one of whom got me a one-year academic exemption when I started CP, while others later kept trying to cancel it…

Parents who were sometimes intrigued but not sufficiently informed, let alone trained…

Trying to understand, explain or even justify the reasons for this state of affairs is most certainly the result of a mind trying to find a reason. A rational explanation.

A cause for this situation.

What scientists commonly call the principle of causality. When a researcher launches a study, he ultimately wants to find a rational cause for what he observes. He has the desire, the will to understand…

I think I'm familiar with this quest for truth… I'm working on it.

Full time!

Even if the etiology of this syndrome is not totally known, the medical community recognizes the evidence of a genetic predisposition, combined with a disorder of the central nervous system and also with early aggression, which may come from environmental factors such as heavy metals, pollution or infectious agents…

Welcome…

Like many people with Asperger's, I have an exceptional memory! Big deal… A vivid memory that never gives birth! Perhaps because, in Socratic maieutics, the maieutician thinks he knows what the *parturient* might give birth to…

So what use is this memory to me?

—To be invaded by insignificant details, even if it's true that it's these that interest me much more than a whole, like the license plates of the family cars I've memorized for over half a century! Faced with a jigsaw puzzle, in order to assemble the various pieces, there are those who observe the image in its entirety and those, the category to which I belong, who will examine each of the different elements in the detail of their cut-outs and memorize them. Figuratively speaking, my story is a bit like a jigsaw puzzle made up of pieces that don't always fit together, and whose links are far from obvious to a Neurotypical mind. Among them, Roland Barthes describes in *Mythologies* that the Citroën DS 19 is "smooth but also the result of elements juxtaposed like a puzzle", that "it obviously falls from the sky" and adds that "it becomes here both more spiritual and more objective"…

Can cars be reincarnated? Where do you sign up?

—Here's to having a general knowledge that allows me to perform at Trivial Poursuit!

But this memory would be more relevant if it were refined, lightened my load and thus enabled me to gain height, to benefit from a more global, more synthetic view, rather than an infinite succession of details buried in tortuous labyrinths that get lost, lost me…

What else?

Mandarin!… Bof!

Damned! Doomed!

What am I guilty of? Is being Asperger's the price I pay for being gifted? A woman doctor confided in me that nature was producing more and more Aspergers because she certainly felt she needed them! A statement she vigorously confirmed, following my remark that more frequent screening favored this increase.

I seem to have understood that, according to Darwinian natural selection, only the offspring best adapted to their environment participate in the next generation. This is how species can evolve and adapt to their environment...

Tare? Avatar?

Hugo Horiot, actor, writer and autistic, declared in *Le Figaro* on March 23, 2018: "Autism is the intelligence of tomorrow."

An interesting hypothesis, even if tomorrow sometimes seems a long way off...

What are we to think of certain parents who find this symptom rewarding, casting *envious* glances at diagnosed Aspergers, and who clumsily try to influence the medical profession, in order to obtain what they think is flattering recognition for their cherubs? Perhaps it's because this syndrome is the subject of so many varied and tainted articles, in which it is sometimes considered to be gifted! Sometimes not! Benefiting from precocity! Sometimes not! An illness? A disability?… Being Asperger's a fad?… Such a pitiful and undignified approach to the plight of each and every person affected!

Fortunately, all the tests, assessments, filmed exercises and interviews are carried out by hyperspecialized doctors, over a period of more than years, and are sufficiently advanced not to fall into the trap of this shameful parental hope!

Life has spoiled me!

Absolutely not in the sense that it fulfilled my every whim, no! rather in the sense that it chose to test me by imposing more or less profound alterations…

So life hasn't spoiled me!

In this context, how does one go about maturing?

If it's recognized that it's not easy to be a human being, I can assure you that it's not always easy to be an Asperger. Intimacy needs esteem to be born and flourish.

And vice versa.

June 2018, I discover my car with a slightly crumpled fender, which is a shame for a Beetle! I contact a professional, but above all an amateur in the original sense of "who loves", so that he can repair it. What I discover is not a garage, but an Ali Baba's cave! A Lotus 2-Eleven type 123, a 1999 Dodge Viper ACR, a Porsche GT2 RS fitted with a Weissach Pack, a Catheram 620R theoretically reserved for the British domestic market… each with its own story told to me by this young enthusiast who doesn't count his time when, he says, he senses that people like beautiful cars!

He won't be disappointed!

He answered every one of my many questions in great detail. My wife, who accompanied me on the return journey, once again proved to be extremely patient… This man of art will admit that I surprised him greatly when I pointed out the Porsche origin of the paintwork on a TVR Tuscan T440R, which did not correspond to the manufacturer's official paintwork! A requirement of the owner, the specialist told me, which disappointed all three of us: the coachbuilder, the car and me!

Excitedly, two days later I returned to pick up my beautifully repaired Beetle, which allowed me to continue my discussion on the cars that were or weren't there. On the following day hand, I'll receive some wonderful photos of the bodywork that this specialist has carried out in carbon, in a Las Vegas garage, on a vintage vehicle, a 1963 Corvette Split Window. How fortunate!

But if I'm asked to talk about the i-Cockpit dashboard of the latest Peugeot 3008, my interest is just as real...

I've never known a single friendly relationship. It's a dimension for which I understand neither the codes nor the purpose. So why don't I have the necessary qualities, the ability to form relationships? Probably because I don't feel the desire or the need to do so. Maybe the other person doesn't really want me as a friend either! Even if they do find us endearing!

As a child, I never brought a single friend home, nor was I invited to the home of a child my own age! I preferred solitude.

Lining up my Norev cars and Dinky Toys, looking at them in minute detail in 1/43 scale, was an exclusive pastime that I loved. Whereas I hated playing soccer as part of a team, or even two-up car racing…

As a teenager, I read a lot, especially philosophy, interspersed with a few bike rides on my own… With a constant interest in cars…

To this day, I confess I still don't have a boyfriend!

What's the point of sharing bread! Especially in the English sense…

The only real relationship I've been able to form outside the family I was born into was magically with my wife. We met at the company that employed us. Her passion and gift for sport impressed me… We began by meeting in stadiums around which we ran…

A personal way of chasing him!

A few sporting escapades, particularly abroad, brought us together for good… We've been married for over thirty-four years.

My wife gave me the confidence I needed. Whatever I've been able to achieve in my life, be it sporting, educational or professional, I've done so because she's been there. Through her contact, I'm aware that I've been able to improve. With what is certainly a colossal margin for progress!

My autonomy is relative!

With subtlety, she gave me all the attention I needed.

The woman who was to become my wife understood me from the first moment we met. I remember how excited I was to dine with her, but also how anxious! As soon as

I was seated in an Italian restaurant, I told her that I was having a little difficulty mastering the art of cutlery. She listened. She smiled. Then we talked about sports and cars… I felt confident.

Simply happy to be here.

As rarely. Like never before.

It was as if destiny had decided on this magnificent and improbable meeting!

There was no way I wasn't going to be able to hold her gaze! I promised myself I'd resist…

His big blue eyes miraculously made me forget everything…

My wife gave me the energy I sorely needed. Generously. The unrestrained energy she gives to everything she does: housework, sport…

She shows me that by being committed to what we do, we can be more serene. It's as if the mind has forgotten that it exists... Peeling vegetables, taking a shower, eating, reading, walking—all soothing activities when practiced with awareness and not control.

I try.

Over and over again...

Watching her live her daily life is a great source of inspiration. Aspiration too. For the best.

She's the only one who understands when I need to go for a run to free myself from present tensions. Or to come...

She alone understands that I can go for weeks, or even much longer, without feeling the urge to go down to our garden.

She's the only one who understands that going to the doctor at is hard for me to bear. All those times when she had to explain to the practitioner that she felt pain in a muscle or a knee when it was mine! We often laughed about it afterwards…

She alone understands my need to wear a body knit. While some people don't leave their jeans behind, I'm faithful to my marcel! In summer, I'm the only one on the beach in a polo shirt under the parasol…

She's the only one who understands that I don't have any friends, not knowing how to be accepted…

She alone understands how important it is for me to have her around, certainly not for base domestic reasons, but because she brings me such a rare sense of affective tive security…

Over the years, my wife has taught me to accept my imperfections, and to embrace the idea that you can be rich in your own cracks. With her, surrendering is not synonymous with giving up. And stepping back doesn't mean taking a step backwards—quite the contrary!

For her part, she says she's thriving in her sporting and family life.

This family, which we've been able to create thanks to her, protects me. Even if there are still some shadows, some embarrassments. These are essentially my fault. Exclusively. Given that, for all these decades, I'm still unable to understand with any certainty the different facial expressions of my loved ones, the atmosphere can sometimes be a little heavy! Mistaking annoyance for benevolence or vice versa is not conducive to getting closer… Just as they are still unable to understand my sometimes disconcerting reactions to a dish I consider too cold…

Hot!

Accepting to be born Asperger's, to be only Asperger's, to live Asperger's, would mean resigning oneself to a life that is nothing but *devastating*. *Devastating*? Be it family, social or professional. To agree to understand the Pantopia only in Pandemonia!

There's speech, the logorrheic flow, even if it means cutting the other off, but also withdrawal, and its corollary boredom… In both cases, oblivion. Of others, of oneself. Of everything.

Mourn the thought of ever being a Neurotypical.

Submit to the idea of having to remain in the night of a NeuroAtypical?

No! But how? What to do?

Hope to give up denial. To anger. Sadness. Firmly resolve to mourn, but fear that you'll remain irremediably glued to the threshold. Lucifer at the center…

As a five-year-old child, I find myself seated at a domini cal luncheon among fifteen or so members of our family. Accustomed to seeing the butter molded with a pretty cow on the top, I was surprised to discover that this time it had a lovely flower on it… I immediately shared my astonishment out loud, asking my grandmother why she bought the butter from the florist? For many years to come, I'd hear the anecdote again and again… Or how pungent mockery can endure beyond the event that raised doubts about parents' ambitious plans for their offspring, and left me feeling extremely uneasy because their sarcasm seemed totally incomprehensible...

Withdrawal into oneself is a phenomenon characteristic of autism, which takes the form of a disinvestment in the world... What's the point of investing? What's in it for me?

As a schoolboy, I wait at the bus stop and observe that on the back of the coaches passing in front of us, the sign reads: "If I wasn't here, you'd have thirty cars instead! I try to share my discovery with my neighbor, telling him that I'd like the bus to break down so that we'd have thirty cars to take us back to our respective homes... His mocking reaction, shouted at the collegiate church, upsets me terribly... hurts me painfully! And now I've decided to keep quiet...

Are the disorders detailed in the autistic triad causes or consequences of this Asperger's condition?

In other words, is keeping silent, shutting oneself away, cutting oneself off from others the syndrome that causes it, or is it a salutary protection against it?

Why let people believe that we could look for the key when we know that there is no lock! That there never will be! You won't find any medication to cure this neurobiological disorder. Doctors have a colossal number of anti-biotic, anti-inflammatory and anti-pain drugs at their disposal, which reassures them... What are they afraid of? Scooping out an Asperger's weirdo for whom there is no anti-Asperger's drug in their pharmacopoeia, or any chemical substance that could restore the beginnings of equilibrium for this disturbed being, so that he feels, if only once in a lifetime, a nanti!

Almost all neurotypicals are familiar with the Cartesian maxim: *Cogito ergo sum* ("I think, therefore I am"). An Aspergerian can't forget the rest: *in arcem meum*, which translates as "in the fortress of my mind". For an Asperger's sufferer, the result is a great deal of torment in the prison of his mind, which is essentially due to who he deeply is, and to all the social injunctions that ask him to forget it. To ignore it…

Resilience is a buzzword which, if transposed into the human sciences, so gnifies that after a trauma, the being has the capacity to live and develop positively. So be it. Basically, the word resilience comes from the physical sciences. It refers to the ability of a physical body to return to its original form after being subjected to a shock, in other words, to return to the way it was before it was deformed. Except that for Aspergers, returning to their original state is certainly not what they want!...

What's in the rear-view mirror of our lives?

This question, which torments many couples, can mean: how did our relationship work out in the first place?

It seems self-evident that my wife and I had to surpass ourselves, as in the words of Ferdinand Porsche: "Surpassing yourself, the only race that never ends. To surpass others seems so elitist, so pretentious. Of course, we can all be ambitious, as long as we draw our energy from potential, but if not, this attitude is often pretentious!

It's worth pointing out that, while for some people this Porsche phrase would have less flavour if it had been uttered by Lada, it's true to say that it can be defined no matter what vehicle life has lent us!

And on a personal level as well as a plural one.

Driver and co-driver. And vice versa.

Like a couple...

It's true that, thanks to my wife's qualities of common sense, we've never been overwhelmed by the situation... She's enabled us to avoid going off the road by negotiating tight bends as best we could, and to succeed in the delicate manoeuvres that life sometimes imposes on us... It's thanks to her that I've been able to deploy forces that I'd never have suspected existed within me, in order to exceed the limits I set myself *a priori*.

Arbitrarily.

Lacanian analysts have a particular interest in the phonetic approach to everything that is expressed. A sort of tic among those who are supposed to treat OCD! And tac by way of re flexion in onomatopoeic form...

My official first name is René. For generations, the first boy in every family has been named René.

Does this mean I can look forward to a saving rebirth? Or has it already happened?

My official middle name is Maurice. When I was a teenager, I decided to call myself René Maurice because I thought it was pure logic to add death to rebirth... The two analysts I had to explain to why I deliberately chose this delightfully oxymoronic grouping of names were very puzzled...

Too bad for me, they didn't even detect my syndrome!

Perhaps because of some skill I sincerely don't know, some people had pretentious designs on my professional career!

On the contrary, they don't know me very well!

I particularly dread :

—annual appraisals, whether in front of a so-called superior or inferior person!

—public speaking engagements, during which people are always ready to torment you openly. Or not!

—breaks at the coffee machine, where people talk about soccer or bad things about those who aren't present…

—exchanges in exclusively vernacular language to insidiously test both your technical knowledge and your membership of the closed circle that is the company… The company which, in law, is considered a "legal person"!… when each human being who makes it up is not considered since it is restrictively referred to as a "physical person"!

—meetings, which are all too often pointless for many of those convened, who often tweet out of spite, sometimes out of defiance...

—lunches, which are generally fake breaks with fake steaks...

That's why I have to admit that I seized the opportunity offered to me to find myself at the head of a very small structure, with the double advantage of only meeting the few staff members furtively, at random in the corridors, and only reporting once a year, when the accounts are released, to shareholders who are very distant... Not only geographically...

When this 42.195-year professional marathon comes to an end, I know that my wife will be waiting for me at the finish line with a radiant smile. My true reward…

I'm neither Neurotypical nor non-Asperger's autistic. I find myself between two worlds so far apart! I can guess them, but I don't really understand them, since I'm different in both cases. Of course, I recognize that the situation of a non-Asperger autistic person is dramatic! But with him, there's no need to pretend. He doesn't hide who he is, he's straightforward!

Entering certain spaces, be they workshops, offices, kitchens, bedrooms, cars, lounges, checkrooms, surgeries, even doctor's surgeries… is often such a mess that it can only make you feel blue! And to imagine being able to empty, structure and tidy up…

What a relief that could be for the place, for the objects! And for me…

I remember that as a child, at the foot of the interior staircase of the family home, there was a jumble of my parents' and my sister's shoes, which had gone up to the bedrooms… I kept lining them up from the smallest to the largest in the direction of descent so, I would tell them, they would be easy to put on… A gesture I performed hundreds of times… In 2010, during a trip to Japan, I had the privilege of staying with my wife and our son in a ryokan. What a pleasure to see all the pairs of shoes correctly positioned! My attraction to the Land of the Rising Sun must have something to do with their very tidy approach to life…

Nature defends its interests. What could be more natural!

If she decides to impose handicaps on some people, perhaps it's by design, so that we can better understand certain problems and try to solve them.

Trisomy affects the twenty-first pair of chromosomes. In addition to the well-known characteristics of this serious handicap, the result is people with a peevish, irascible disposition. Since nature doesn't like disorder, every cell in this body is disturbed by this third chromosome and fights against it, trying to expel it. It's a losing battle, and a particularly grueling one!

Similarly, every cell in the human body has twenty-two pairs of homologous chromosomes and one pair of sex chromosomes. In men, the sex-defining chromosome pair is made up of an X and a Y chromosome, whereas in women, each cell of the body harmoniously contains only forty-six X chromosomes divided into twenty-three pairs. See the often excited, nervous man, whose life expectancy is more than seven years shorter than that of the woman, could perhaps find a reading in this disturbance within each of his cells! Nature, not liking what is lacking, would never cease to fight against what seems disharmonious.

How then, in this admittedly simplistic approach, can we not be tempted to make a link with the genetic anomalies detected in Asperger's and non-Asperger's autistic people, when we know that autism affects four men for every woman? With the DNA at the heart of each chromosome, described as a messenger? And partially interpreted by nature as a kind of waste product?

Perhaps the beginnings of an understanding of the withdrawal, anger and fatigue seen in some Asperger's and non-Asperger's autistic people?

In the same vein, what message is to be understood from the genes of the two Neurotypic parents that would become toxic by combining? And give birth to a *Neologism*… Himself having had the good fortune to be the father of a Neurotypical, without ever having been aware of the slightest potential risk of transmission for his filiation…

Even if the idea of heredity is linked to that of a caste, and can thus correspond to a group of individuals united by the same origin, such as a disease, autistic people cannot belong to any dedicated caste, since each one of them is just a casting error! A specialist doctor told me that the contribution of Aspergers to the understanding of autism has been decisive in recent years.

Brilliant!

Tonight, a soccer match on TV as part of the World Cup in Russia! That's all anyone's talking about. Except for me...

While I understand the rules of refereeing, I don't understand this craze at all! This delirious passion... I feel like a stranger to all this agitation, this frenzy... Very often I'm asked to keep quiet...

When it comes to repair surfaces... I imagine the mechanic arriving in overalls, with his tool kit...

"I pity those who look intelligent, it's a promise we can't keep", Alain's phrase in his *Propos sur l'esthétique*, appeals to me for several reasons.

In the French language, intelligence and intellectuel have their first six letters in common... Is that enough to lump them together? It's a reductive misunderstanding that causes a great deal of frustration, even though intelligence is certainly not exclusively intellectual. Etymologically, it comes from the Latin *intellegere*, meaning the faculty of understanding. Thus defined, everyone can know a che min intelligent singular...

Intelligence expresses itself fabulously at the level of the heart. It's an intelligence full of subtleties, a purity of feeling that comes from the nobility of the soul, like the generosity that inhabits so many wonderful people. A generosity that is not exclusively material, and that consists of giving sometimes more than we possess. On the other hand, the soul's *ignobility* is mostly a matter of stupidity, such as that which consists in speaking of those who are absent, all too often in unflattering terms! Intelligence is also to be found in a practical dimension, in creativity and ingenuity, as exemplified by cooks, gardeners, mothers and fathers, or automotive engineers … All of whom are in the *creative business*.

The ideal situation would of course be to have all three intelligences in harmonious balance, with the added bonus of a strong amplitude…

Let's digress for a moment to the cognitive sciences, where we find artificial intelligence, which, in a simplistic approach, represents all the theories and techniques capable of simulating human intelligence. Or even to stimulate it… It proposes to solve highly complex problems. To do this, it uses artificial neural networks like algorithms; metamathematics, i.e. mathematics as a language; and computer science, in its conceptual and concrete dimensions.

For this last dimension, quantum computing has recently come into its own, making it possible to carry out operations not involving the classical manipulation of bits in a Manichean state of 1 or 0, but of qubits, which means carrying out fantastic manipulations in a state of 1 and 0 at the same time, and thus defining the concept of entanglement.

Quite simply, for classical computing, there is only black and white, but for quantum computing, thanks to black and white, there is grey! That of matter… And in the future, which is certainly more literary than calendrical, we'll probably have an even wider palette of colors at our disposal…

Quite a program…

So, thanks to this revolutionary contribution, we can imagine and hope for cross-disciplinary, unconventional, non-conformist, synesthetic solutions, between human beings, to challenges such as illness, death.… Disability…

But before we close this certainly very promising parenthesis, let's evoke the Promethean myth, by re-reading Hans Jonas who, in *The Responsibility Principle*, highlights the risks incurred by technical choices that can unbalance life in general, and human life in particular… Above all, let's avoid slipping from transhumanism to *trashumanism* by trying to impose that morality ensures that this artificial intelligence can only function if it is managed equitably by the three human intelligences previously mentioned…

Finally, why shouldn't there be another form of intelligence, a spiritual one this time (in which ritual is central, as it is in the life of every Asperger…), free or not from religious faith, which could prove to be a harmonious and inspiring faculty of understanding? Aspiring for the other three intelligences, and who would be the supreme knacker… A soul, come to improve itself here on earth in a skin… and a mind imposed, inherited, *mherited*? And who would then rise up there, finally rid of its container and its contents that have become too cumbersome, enriched by its diverse and varied experiences, such as those of being a Asperger… or not.

Meaningful experiences only if they were actually lived, and not on the Internet, and if acts in kind are potentially neutral, the intention attributed to them is always decisive…

A kind of absolute transcendence that would imply an immanence of experience…

Thoughts that are both ascensional and *assertional*, and which obviously only commit the author, as with any type of reasoning that is not provable, but perhaps just intuitive…

Of all the colors, blue is my favorite. I recently learned that it's a constant in Asper ger. Whether it concerns eyes, clothes, shutters, cars, the sky or the sea, it has always been my reference color.

I'd like to see blue everywhere… I see it everywhere! Especially in English! Blues being synonymous with nostalgia, gloom and melancholy…

I just wish I could eat them. If all colors can be represented on a plate with a wide panel, it seems impossible to enjoy a dish with the color blue… Even if it is cited for cooking certain meats, it doesn't correspond to any reality…

Parbleu! Chefs, to your brushes…

Live permanently with great rigidity.

Physically. Psychologically. Socially. Intellectually…

Clumsy. Left, center. Everywhere.

I love to run. For a long time. Always on the same asphalt course. I love to smell the asphalt under the sun that softens it, under the rain that washes it… A la Forrest…

Zatopek said: "If you want to run, run a kilometer. If you want to change your life, run a marathon." I started with a half. Then marathons. Then hundred kilometers, forty-eight hours, six days… For these two durations, I was told in 2012 that I had been ranked twenty-first at my dial in my age category! A one-kilometre tarmac track to run in a loop for six days and five nights, with my wife in support.

What a foot for over five hundred and thirty laps!

Some say I'm persevering... I admit I don't like failure in what I do, which means accepting to run sometimes with painful periostitis...

I'd like to be able to run all the time... Not in order to boastfully display a VIP bellybag! Not to risk bigorexia and runner's high! Just to run and escape. From myself...

Perhaps the worst prison is the one without bars? I got life in absentia, but what's my crime? Was there a seated jury, a standing plea, a terrifying deliberation?

Neighbors tell me they see me often, everywhere, running and running! That they recognize me from afar, with that very personal stride! Very characteristic of a style not à la Jump but à la Gump...

As a child, how many times did I hear my father tell me to walk with my heel rather than my toe! In fact, what he expected of me was impossible…

When I went into National Service, I found myself working in an office at the General Staff. I'm sure there weren't many of us who would have performed so pitifully in the initial "marching in step" training!

How can you imagine that I've been skiing for a few days every year, for over four decades, and that only the stem with planted poles allows me to ski down clear blue slopes! I only know three runs in a gigantic ski area, and my wife is still amazed to see me skiing down them with turns negotiated in exactly the same place!

My wife strongly advises against cycling with automatic pedals! Not to say forbidden!

The special cleat attached to the bottom of the shoe, which clicks onto the pedal so that both rider and bike are attached, is not suitable for someone as greedy as me! I must admit I've already experienced some pretty ridiculous attempts…

Nothing beats the classic pedals, which I can lose without too much risk!

Of course, I'm somewhat aware that this physical rigidity is also expressed through its synonyms in other dimensions: austerity, stiffness, intransigence, gravity, hardness… Great clumsiness…

Without ever hoping to know the antonyms: abandonment, softness, suppleness, elasticity… When I stumble, which is quite often, my reflex is to put my arms back… with the damage I display as discreetly as possible…

Figuratively speaking too!

Summer 2016, on a stretch of the GR20 in Corsica, I'm walking in front of my wife when I bump into a pebble at minus three centimetres high! I start off with my head forward, arms back, pushed by the weight of my rucksack. This must be what we call a glide! Just as I hear my wife shouting "Careful!", I feel my fist thump against hard reality! Nothing broken! Just a little smashed… My wife seems once again puzzled by my disconcerting reflex to throw my arms back when I lose my balance…

I think this damned clumsiness has been with me for a very long time. I have distant memories of jam jars that only a neighbor, called to the rescue by my mother, was able to open… Or in secondary school, during handicraft classes, in pottery for example, when the teacher had to get personally involved in my sketches to limit breakage, all the while muttering that he found me particularly clumsy!

The difficulty of being integrated into society, of living among men and women for whom verbal exchange is the starting point. For me, the stumbling block.

In discussions in my presence, I often manage to understand the ins and outs, but I'm often totally indifferent to the subject matter. That's why I'm always waiting for the crucial moment when I can talk about something that interests me, something I'm passionate about, rather than giving my point of view. Cars, for example…

And if that opportunity doesn't present itself quickly enough, I cut myself off to explain my subject… Which has the merit of annoying my one-night-only audience (with yet another excessive possessive,

I agree!), especially as I don't let go of my text easily and this audience is, in spite of itself, in spite of me, either obliged to suffer my words, or to find a pretext for a premature departure… All the more so as my flow of words has always been of a sustained rhythm, perhaps because a rapid elocution allows me to conceal, even partially, the expression of my emotions?

In the same vein, the phrase "to drink someone's words" is a statement that doesn't come naturally to me! Nevertheless, after trying to go beyond the literal meaning, I thought I understood what fluidity in a presentation positively means. In this case, the words are so limpid that they can fill any container. Each one receiving a content that marvelously matches the receptacle offered. But in my case, my flow is so uncontrolled that, whatever the container in front of me, a significant part of the stream of my words gushing out with force, in jerks, hits the walls and ends up on the outside. Lost.

The recipient feeling splashed...

Sprayed by an Asperger's!

To the people I confided my ASD to, reactions were mixed. There were those who told me they only saw it as confirmation of what they thought I was, those who refused to express themselves, those who never stopped asking me about this syndrome, or those who imagined me born on a blue day, or singing in the rain like Rain Man, synesthetic or even able to recite the first ten thousand digits of Pi...

Yes, the commonly accepted criteria fit me, but contrary to popular belief, we're not all Bill Gates or George Lucas. Nor are all

Neurotypicals Albert Einstein or Mstislav Rostropovitch… I'm one Asperger among many Aspergers.

In fact, I've told very few people that I'm Asperger's…

Don't tell my mother or my father that I'm Asperger's. They only think I have a few abilities… Especially as they belong to a generation that did not hesitate, wrongly, to give responsibility to the mothers of autistic children!

No ethics! And even if it was a small label, stuck on the backs of the mothers designated as guilty, even though they often turned out to be outstanding mothers, it had dramatic repercussions for those directly concerned: autistic children.

Articles dealing with Asperger's often mention a depressive dimension, and sometimes the hypothesis of a temptation to leave early…

The latter being the consequence of the former!

When I come into contact with another person who, in spite of himself, puts pressure on me to be like him, plus the pressure I put on myself to act as if, depression can find fertile ground in me… Here too, I have to resist. Which isn't always easy, because it aggravates the symptom…

As for autolysis, although I verbally considered it once or twice a long time ago with those around me in situations that I perhaps wrongly perceived as abandonment, I've decided to get rid of this odious idea of blackmail. I now find it indecent. Like everyone else, I've signed a lease for this life without knowing how long it will last.

It's up to him to answer the three essential questions: where? when? how?

It's up to me to hope I can tell him what I think…

The couple my wife and I form is a hybrid, combining two engines with different energies. If skeptics need reassurance, its longevity bears witness to the fact that it's possible to move forward together, whatever the original conditions, whatever our way of life… And if a breakdown of any kind occurs in our relationship, my wife believes that this pause forces us to try and better understand how we function. Which translates into car language: as long as things are running smoothly, we don't ask ourselves any questions! It's only when a car is at a standstill that we start trying to understand how it works…

I was born Asperger's.

I will die with Asperger's.

This is my life.

If some people are committed to life, I'm mostly caged!

Autism Spectrum Disorder accompanies me day after day. Night after night.

It leaves me little space... Are we united for better? For worse?

Knowing that I'm completely unable to imagine what my life would have been like if I hadn't been affected by this syndrome!

Nor for those around me...

If you look at it from the outside, the picture of my life seems attractive.

A nice family with a loving wife, a blossoming son and affectionate parents.

A decent job.

Regular exercise, including some interesting competitions, which suggests that I'm in good health…

If you look with an inner eye (hello squint!) and try to focus on what my life is like, far from being a false ass, am I a happy person?…

If only serene?

Sorry if I'm boring you with all my questions…

Especially as I'm not sure that I have the right answers.

But rather the wrong ones…

Because that's what goes on in an Asperger's head! If I'm *intrusive*, I find that it's all too often the wrong positions that prevail. Which express themselves spontaneously.

Like this propensity to grumble! A real talent in this area…

Why is that?

Maybe because deep down, deep inside, I'd really like to be rid of the weight of this syndrome.

What weighs on me are all the ridiculous, pointless efforts I make on a daily basis, which take me away from reality. From the present moment. From myself. From each other.

Dissatisfied with my situation, grumbling is an absurdly easy way out…

Escape?

Probably…

Grumbling because I too often find myself unable to understand that it's utopian to wait for everything to be perfect before hoping for peace and quiet?

Whereas if I even conceived the idea of being quiet, events would certainly be more likely to unfold correctly…

Not easy…

I absolutely do not consider this writing as a testimony. Because that term implies a witness, and therefore a not wise witness. And I refuse to pass this witness on to anyone. Who would want it anyway? Who would want to take over?

I'd rather stay alone on the track, relentlessly turning lap after lap…

But what to do now with this diagnosis?

First of all, we must avoid falling into the distressing naivety of thinking that it's enough to name the disease for it to cease to exist. Diagnosis doesn't explain everything. Nor does it solve everything.

I'd rather remember William Shakespeare's suggestion in *The Merry Wives of Windsor* (act V, scene v): "*What cannot be eschwe'd must be embrac'd…*"

Unable to escape this syndrome within me, which is me, all that's left is to hope:

—To embrace what I am deep down, in my foundations, basics, fundamentals, an Asperger. The verb "to embrace" is to be taken in a figurative sense, not in the sense of "to fuck"!

—To obtain the forgiveness of all those I may have hurt, even if very often it was essentially through this clumsiness which is one of my most striking signatures!

—*Moderate* myself, but without over-molesting myself...

—To become permanently aware of the relativity of my worries.

—Accept the situation.

—As a lover of cars, try to play a little with the one of derision rather than tirelessly with the one of criticism...

Of course, this realization is not so sudden, but rather the result of a long process of maturation that follows on from the existential questioning that has characterized me for so long! The diagnosis proved to be the catalyst.

In *The Myth of Sisyphus*, which I've read several times and which recounts the life of the man who dared to defy Thanatos, the personification of Death, this hero's absurd life boils down to tirelessly pushing a boulder to the top of a mountain, which rolls inexorably down the valley, just before reaching the hoped-for goal. Despite the stupidity of this obligation, Albert Camus asks us to imagine Sisyphus happy! Because the Camusian Sisyphus is not focused on the aberration of what he has to achieve, but just on making it happen. Nothing else. Forget the meaning of what he's doing, just do it.

Trying to *camusisyphier* myself by trying to forget what it means to be Asperger's but live it. Fully…

Of course, I admit I'm relieved that specialized doctors have been able to put a word to this affliction that has characterized me since birth. Knowing that other human beings live with this syndrome in no way diminishes my day-to-day worries. Having researched this syndrome, having responded to the numerous requests from the medical profession and therefore being recognized as an Asperger's sufferer certainly enables me to understand a little better who I am, and *the same goes* for those around me, so that they reject me less, and thus feel less ostracized.

Asperger's and I are intimate. A *team*?

Definitely not a *dream team*… And who's the *team leader*?

It's a pity that this diagnosis can't be aimed at every single person I've ever met in my life, nor at those I'm going to meet now, because she com would finally understand why I sometimes seem a bit strange! Of course, "man-sandwiching" myself doesn't seem to be a satisfactory solution either, because going from being closeted to being closeted, what a destabilizing upheaval that would cause!

Knowing that this recognition is a reality is the beginning of comfort and appeasement…

Thanks to the combination of this diagnosis with the inevitable process of erosion, those around me have told me that they have noticed that the anger has gradually lost its power, often turning into irritability, and sometimes even slipping into the more subdued form of muted irritation!

Decrescendo-do...

My wife forgave every one of my mistakes. Forgot my failures. Overcame my fragility. Accepted my routines with kindness. With understanding. Spared me the tension.

Her tolerance and indulgence fostered the emergence of abilities in me. Without her, I would certainly have lamented my relative inabilities.

She reassured me, gave me confidence by showing me the essence of who I am, and not who I think I am.

She is so precious to me, as when she teaches me that far from the turpitudes of the mind, when the heart is right, everything is right... In fact, the diagnosis didn't teach her anything she didn't already know. She just subtly asked me not to talk about it any more, fearing that I'd get locked into regressive thoughts.

Here again, I know she's right.

That her advice is good.

Because she knows me.

She really does. She's a balm for a mind as stressed and tense as mine. She knows how to reconnect me to what's essential when I'm rambling. When I'm feeling light-headed. The *soul tsunami…*

It's so important that she's accepted me as I am. For never judging me. For appreciating my quirky side. That sets me apart.

Part of my charm, as she sometimes says…

For a relatively long time now, I've been aware of being troubled by the suffering felt by the living world, particularly that which belongs to the organic kingdom: be it animal or vegetable. More than a hundred times a year, equipped with a plastic cap and a cardboard box, I capture flying insects, doomed to certain death because they are trapped behind glass. Freeing them and watching them fly away seems to redeem me…

Similarly, after the recent violent storms, I delicately and discreetly replanted fallen shrubs and, when hiking, I try to avoid trampling the vegetation, even if it means taking very long detours… As for humans, it's life's wounded that arouse my interest. Mostly children. And if I can't always find the right look, gesture or word, I feel like I'm not a stranger to them.

In fact, I'm drawn to each and every one of these many suffering beings.

In the film *Dolls* by Japanese director Takeshi Kitano, which we saw with our son when it was released, couples who pass through the four seasons are linked by a red rope. The central theme of the film, with its subtle aesthetics, is *bunraku*, a type of Japanese theater in which the characters are large puppets manipulated on sight... Beyond Yojhi Yamamoto's sublime costumes, where some see in this work a kind of ode to renunciation, we retained the symbolism of this link that unites each of the couples and which is quite simply exceptional.

This bond can be materialized by our wireless telephone contacts, which enable us to call each other to make sure they've arrived for their appointment, or to let us know they've left their gym class or jogging session... Far from intrusive control, the pleasure of simply exchanging with my wife gives me a real sense of delight every time... And what a relief it is when I see her hurry back to the villa because she too has realized she's forgotten her smartphone, our faithful link!

October 2017.

My wife and our son take part for the third year running in a mountain bike competition, this time on a new course. At my request, depending on the weather conditions, their respective training sessions, the difficulty of the event and the quality of their equipment, they plan to take around 3 hours to cross the finish line.

The first upset came when my son called to tell me he'd had a technical problem that would delay him by thirty minutes.

Once across the line, he recovers from his efforts. After briefly asking him about his race, I return to my place just a few metres from the finish line to welcome my wife, who in theory should be here any minute…

Then the waiting. A long wait. Horribly agonizing. Even worse than the waits at the doctor's surgery or the post office…

My son calls me on the phone to tell me that he's fifty meters away from me and is watching me walk in circles, describing me as if I'd turned into some kind of dromaniac locked in a virtual cage! He reproaches me for not sending out any positive vibes for his mother and for selfishly thinking only of my expectations, only of myself…

I feel an enormous tension.

Keeping watch seems inordinately endless!

My son, whom I keep questioning, finally sets off to meet his mother , who arrives some thirty minutes later than originally planned. Smiles on their faces… Not me…

They are both legitimately exhausted by the great effort they have put into this sporting event. I'm exhausted by what I've just been through!

Back to the villa, quick showers, then a hasty departure at my request in order to be on time to celebrate their performance in a restaurant. Probably because I'm exhausted from the day's upsets, my wife and our son admit to being disappointed when I seem to be discourteous with some of my table neighbors, who have asked me about the terrace heating and to whom I haven't deigned to reply... Then shortly afterwards, the two sportsmen, who are debriefing their errands, point out that I keep interrupting them to talk about other subjects..., particularly cars....

Over and over again, the same old torments! Will it never end?

But why on earth did Sisyphus provoke Thanatos?

The Rolling Stones would be well advised to play *Out Of Our Heads* over and over again… in my head…

The leading family association, Vaincre l'autisme, puts forward a few key figures in support of INSERM (Institut national de la santé et de la recherche médicale): "Every day, the figures on autism become more alarming. Much remains to be discovered… However, it is already certain that autism represents a real public health challenge, to which there is an urgent need to respond.

—1 in 100 births affected by ASD (Autism Spectrum Disorder)

—650,000 people affected in France, according to internationally recognized prevalences.

—ASD affects 4 boys for every 1 girl.

—Around half of those affected by ASD also have an intellectual disability (IQ below 70).

—According to recent estimates, around 1% of the British and American populations suffer from ASD. This suggests that as many as 5 million people in the European Union are affected.

—In France, partial and non-adapted care costs a minimum of 2,500 euros per child per month, a financial burden essentially borne by the child's family.

—80% of children with autism in France do not attend school

—37% of French people wrongly believe that autism is a psychological disorder (Opinion Way survey, 2012)

—61% of French people believe that there are around 50,000 people affected by autism in France… instead of 650,000!

—The consequences on human lives are priceless…"

The sooner autism is detected, the sooner the diagnosed person, especially a non-adult, will have the opportunity to be cared for by dedicated teams, and his or her entourage supported. What I would have appreciated for my family. And for me. Knowing that I'm well aware of how lucky I've been to share my life with someone as caring and devoted as my wife.

A large number of children and adults, older and younger, are unaware that they are affected by this syndrome, and a diagnosis could represent the beginning of progress for everyone: a real relief for the person concerned and those who consider him or her… Working for this cause, however modestly, can be a motivating challenge.

This booklet, in which I've tried to give my all, is just the beginning. It's a writing of hope for a better life. For everyone...

If I have the reputation of liking to tidy up, perhaps it's just a subterfuge to avoid being considered deranged! And need I say it, I don't see myself ever tidying up cars!

However, as much as my writings and files are classified, ordered, hierarchized and thematized, this time I preferred the spontaneity that keeps self-censorship at bay!

Putting myself together without correcting myself...

Don't *litter* me, dare to deligot me!

So I opted for a text of 14,101 words, with the aim, as initially expressed, of introducing you to my syndrome through a sort of miscellany that reveals, I believe, who I am fundamentally, inwardly, intimately, so that you can be at closer, even for a very brief moment, to the mind of an Asperger's sufferer…

If you have even the slightest doubt about yourself or another person, dare to take the plunge, dare to speak out, dare to meet specialists… So that one day you may be able to smile, because at last you are simply understood and accepted in your uniqueness.

That smile that everyone hopes for, that everyone secretly dreams of…

Asperger's or not…

Best sellers Max Milo Editions

The Russian Art of War
Jacques Baud

Hitler's Banker
Jean-François Bouchard

Confessions of a forger
Éric Piedoie Le Tiec

The Koran and the Flesh
Ludovic-Mohamed Zahed

Governing by Fake News
Jacques Baud

Governing by Chaos
Lucien Cerise

A Political History of Food
Paul Ariès

Mad in U.S.A.: T
he Ravages of the "American Model"
Michel Desmurget

Mondial Soccer Club Geopolitics
Kévin Veyssière

Putin: Game Master?
Jacques Baud

Treatise on the Three Impostors:
Moses, Jesus, Muhammad
The Spirit of Spinoza

TV Lobotomy
Michel Desmurget